THE DAYTONA 500

T0014966

BY ANNETTE M. CLAYTON

Apex is distributed by North Star Editions:
sales@northstareditions.com | 888-417-0195

Produced for Apex by Red Line Editorial.

Photographs ©: Phelan M. Ebenhack/AP Images, cover; Shutterstock Images, 1, 4–5, 6–7, 15, 16–17, 18–19, 20–21, 24, 26, 27, 29; John Raoux/AP Images, 8–9; AP Images, 10–11, 12–13; James P. Kerlin/AP Images, 14; Chris O'Meara/AP Images, 22–23; Arthur Grace/Zuma Press/Newscom, 25

Library of Congress Control Number: 2022912063

ISBN
978-1-63738-290-5 (hardcover)
978-1-63738-326-1 (paperback)
978-1-63738-396-4 (ebook pdf)
978-1-63738-362-9 (hosted ebook)

Printed in the United States of America
Mankato, MN
012023

NOTE TO PARENTS AND EDUCATORS

Apex books are designed to build literacy skills in striving readers. Exciting, high-interest content attracts and holds readers' attention. The text is carefully leveled to allow students to achieve success quickly. Additional features, such as bolded glossary words for difficult terms, help build comprehension.

TABLE OF CONTENTS

CHAPTER 1

DRIVERS, START YOUR ENGINES!

Race cars speed around the Daytona International Speedway. Drivers fight for the lead. It's the first few laps of the Daytona 500.

During races, NASCAR drivers reach speeds of up to 200 miles per hour (322 km/h).

Pit crews often replace tires during pit stops.

Some cars' tires shred. Fuel also runs low. Each driver's **pit crew** is ready to help. They work fast to fix the cars.

PIT STOP

Most people take 20 minutes to change car tires. NASCAR pit crews are much faster. They can do it in less than 20 seconds!

Austin Cindric (2) finishes ahead of Bubba Wallace (23) to win the 2022 Daytona 500.

On the last lap, cars compete to finish first. But one car keeps the lead. This car speeds across the finish line to win the race.

FAST FACT

The Daytona 500 is 500 miles (805 km) long. Drivers complete 200 laps around the track.

CHAPTER 2

DAYTONA HISTORY

Early NASCAR races took place at Daytona Beach in Florida. Part of the racetrack ran along the shore.

Cars get ready to start a NASCAR race at Daytona Beach, Florida, in 1956.

In 1959, the race moved to the Daytona International Speedway. This was the first Daytona 500.

Lee Petty (42) finished the 1959 Daytona 500 just ahead of Johnny Beauchamp (73).

PHOTO FINISH

The first Daytona 500 had a photo finish. Two cars crossed the finish line together. Judges studied a photo of the cars for three days. They decided Lee Petty was the winner.

Early race cars were boxy. Over time, race cars became **sleek**. This shape made them faster. The Daytona 500 also got more popular. Thousands of fans came to watch it each year.

Early race cars had doors that could fly open during races. Drivers could get hurt.

Today's race cars have no doors. Drivers climb in through the window.

FAST FACT

Millions of people watch the Daytona 500 on TV every year.

CHAPTER 3

RACING RULES

The Daytona 500 is part of the NASCAR Cup Series. That's the top level for **stock car** racing.

The Daytona 500 is nicknamed "The Great American Race."

The race includes 40 cars. First, cars race one at a time. They take turns doing one lap. The fastest two cars earn front-row spots.

FAST FACT

The fastest single-car time wins the pole position. This is the front row and inside of the track.

Starting in the pole position makes it easier for a driver to win the race.

Duel races decide the rest of the order. Drivers race 60 laps. Faster cars will start ahead of slower ones.

Drivers compete for top spots during a duel race for the 2021 Daytona 500.

OPEN TEAMS

Most Cup Series drivers are guaranteed a spot at Daytona. But four spots are open. Two drivers can get in through their single-car times. And two make it through the duels.

CHAPTER 4

DYNAMITE DRIVERS

D ale Earnhardt was one of the greatest NASCAR drivers. But it took him 20 tries to win Daytona. He finally won it in 1998.

In 2001, Dale Earnhardt died in a car crash. Fans hold up three fingers for him. This was his car number.

Earnhardt's son had more success. Dale Earnhardt Jr. won Daytona in 2004 and 2014. Richard Petty won seven times between 1964 and 1981. That is still the most ever.

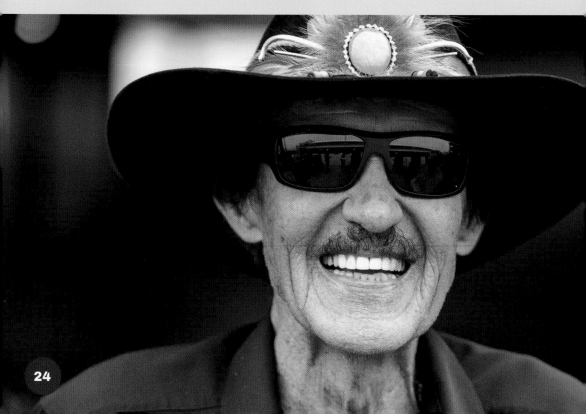

Richard Petty is known as "The King." He is one of the greatest NASCAR drivers ever.

BREAKING BARRIERS

In 1963, Wendell Scott became the first Black driver in the Daytona 500. Janet Guthrie was the first woman at Daytona. She raced in 1977.

Janet Guthrie raced in NASCAR's Cup Series from 1976 to 1978. She also raced in two events in 1980.

In 2016, Denny Hamlin set the record for the closest finish. He also won back-to-back in 2019 and 2020.

In 2016, Denny Hamlin trailed in Daytona's last lap. But he pulled ahead to win by just 0.11 seconds.

In 2021, Bubba Wallace became the first Black driver to lead a lap at Daytona.

FAST FACT

Danica Patrick led a lap at Daytona in 2013. She was the first woman to do so.

COMPREHENSION QUESTIONS

Write your answers on a separate piece of paper.

1. Write a paragraph that explains the main ideas of Chapter 2.

2. Would you want to race in the Daytona 500? Why or why not?

3. How many Daytona 500s did Richard Petty win?

    A. two

    B. three

    C. seven

4. How does winning the duel race help drivers during the Daytona 500?

    A. It means they start the race ahead of other cars.

    B. It means they win the pole position.

    C. It means they can also race in next year's Daytona 500.

5. What does compete mean in this book?

On the last lap, cars compete to finish first.
But one car keeps the lead.

   A. to fix a car
   B. to start a race
   C. to try to beat others

6. What does popular mean in this book?

The Daytona 500 also got more popular.
Thousands of fans came to watch it each year.

   A. not known to most people
   B. liked by many people
   C. hard to find

Answer key on page 32.

GLOSSARY

duel races
Two 60-lap, 150-mile (241-km) races that take place before the Daytona 500 to decide which drivers will take part in the race and the order in which they will start.

guaranteed
Happening no matter what.

NASCAR
Short for "National Association for Stock Car Auto Racing." NASCAR is the largest US racing organization.

photo finish
The end of a race that is so close people must study a photo of it to tell who won.

pit crew
A team of people who fix cars during a race.

sleek
Having a shape that cuts through the air.

stock car
A type of race car that has the frame of a regular car but has other powerful parts for racing.

TO LEARN MORE

BOOKS

Adamson, Thomas K. *Stock Cars*. Minneapolis: Bellwether Media, 2019.

Doeden, Matt. *Stock Cars*. North Mankato, MN: Capstone Press, 2019.

Schlesinger, Emily. *Racetracks*. Costa Mesa, CA: Saddleback Educational Publishing, 2019.

ONLINE RESOURCES

Visit www.apexeditions.com to find links and resources related to this title.

ABOUT THE AUTHOR

Annette M. Clayton enjoys hiking on the Appalachian Trail, reading, and writing books for kids. She lives in Maryland with her husband and twin daughters. Her favorite sport to watch is soccer.

INDEX

ANSWER KEY:
1. Answers will vary; 2. Answers will vary; 3. C; 4. A; 5. C; 6. B